G000135461

Purple Ronnie's
Star Signs

Aries

21st March - 20th April

☆

First published 1994 by Statics (London) Ltd

This edition published 2002 by Boxtree
an imprint of Pan Macmillan Ltd
Pan Macmillan, 20 New Wharf Road, London N1 9RR
Basingstoke and Oxford
Associated companies throughout the world
www.panmacmillan.com

ISBN 0 7522 2042 X

9 8 7 6 5 4 3 2 1

A CIP catalogue record for this book is available from
the British Library

Text by Giles Andreae
Illustrations by Janet Cronin
Printed and bound in Hong Kong

21st March - 20th April
ARIES
Ariens fancy Leo and Sagittarius

☆ Introduction ☆

Star Signs are a brilliant way of finding out about someone's character. You can use them to discover anything you like including what everyone's secretest rude fantasies are.

But reading what's written in the stars can only be done by incredibly brainy people like me. After gazing for ages through my gigantic telescope and doing loads of complicated sums an charts and stuff I have been able to work out exactly what everyone in the world is really like.

This book lets you know about all my amazing discoveries. It tells you what you look like, who your friends are, how your love life is, what you're like at Doing It and who you should be Doing It with.

Everything I've written in this book is completely true. Honest.

Love from

Purple Ronnie

xox

Contents

They like to be saucy
and daring

And love to find trouble
and danger

So talk about bosoms in
front of their Mums

And show off their
bottoms to strangers

Cor blimey!

Aries Looks

Aries people have a fun
and happy look as if they
are bubbling over with life.
As soon as you look at an
Aries they think you
fancy them

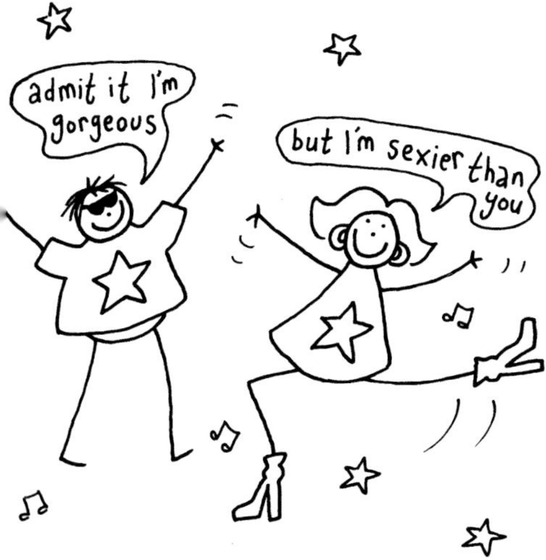
admit it I'm gorgeous
but I'm sexier than you

Aries Men

Aries Men are strong and sexy. They have big bottoms and feet like plates. Their tongues often hang out and sometimes they dribble

Aries Women

Aries Women have a saucy way of looking at you. They have friendly smiles, sparkling eyes and they like wearing sexy outfits

crack

Aries Character

Ariens are great fun to be with cos they love

action and adventure
and they always think up
crazy ideas

Aries people love competitions and they get very cross and grumpy

f you don't let them
win at everything

Aries and Friends

An Aries always has loads of friends for getting pissed with and partying all night long

"
slurp
"

Danger:- NEVER tell an Aries what to do

or they will shout and scream and kick you in the goolies

Aries people would be good at being...

1. They love bossing everyone around and telling them what to do

2. They are great at making clever plans

verybody listen to my super genius plan
SNOGGING TACTICS
A- find girl
B- give girl masses of booze
C- tell girl she is v. sexy
D - Snog girl

3. They are very brave and like nothing better than a good battle

Aries and Love

Secretly Ariens are worried
that they're useless so you
must tell them how
gorgeously smashing
and lovely they are
all the time

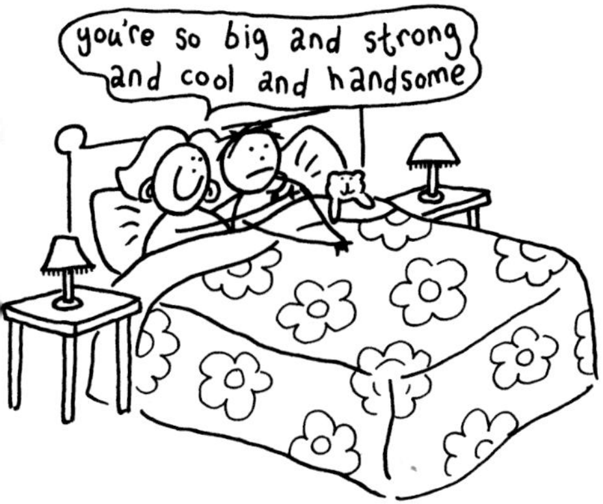
you're so big and strong and cool and handsome

Warning:- Always try to be as mysterious as possible or your Aries might run off with somebody else

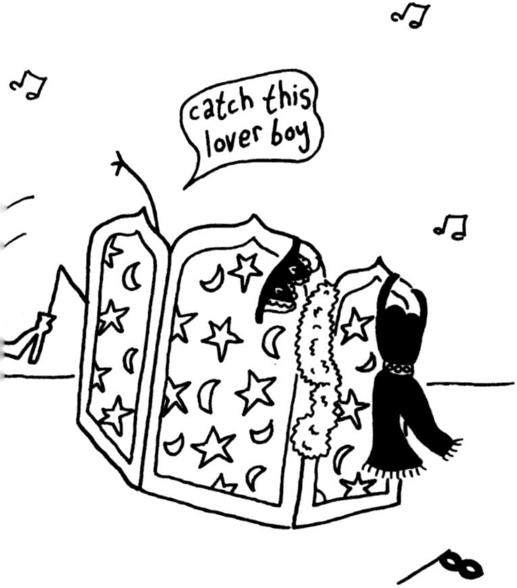
catch this lover boy

Most of the time
love with an
Aries is fun and
mad and very
exciting

Aries and Sex

Ariens are completely sex-mad.

They love Doing It in all sorts of places at any time of the day

⭐ Secret Tip ⭐

Aries people love the chase...

.. so you must never give in
to them too quickly

Arien women love being on top and most of them eat men for breakfast

The End